All About Food Crops

# APPLES

Cecelia H. Brannon

**Enslow Publishing**
101 W. 23rd Street
Suite 240
New York, NY 10011
USA

enslow.com

Published in 2018 by Enslow Publishing, LLC
101 W. 23rd Street, Suite 240, New York, NY 10011

**Library of Congress Cataloging-in-Publication Data**

Names: Brannon, Cecelia H., author. | Brannon, Cecelia H. All about food crops.
Title: Apples / Cecelia H. Brannon.
Description: New York, NY : Enslow Publishing, 2018. | Series: All about food crops | Audience: Pre-K to grade 1. | Includes bibliographical references and index.
Identifiers: LCCN 2017002019| ISBN 9780766085756 (library-bound) | ISBN 9780766088269 (pbk.) | ISBN 9780766088207 (6-pack)
Subjects: LCSH: Apples—Juvenile literature.
Classification: LCC SB363 .B69 2018 | DDC 634/.11—dc23
LC record available at https://lccn.loc.gov/2017002019

Printed in the United States of America

**To Our Readers:** We have done our best to make sure all websites in this book were active and appropriate when we went to press. However, the author and the publisher have no control over and assume no liability for the material available on those websites or on any websites they may link to. Any comments or suggestions can be sent by email to customerservice@enslow.com.

# Contents

# Words to Know

applesauce

cider

orchard

Apples are an important crop.

There are many different kinds of apples. Some apples are red. Some are green. Some are yellow.

Apples grow on trees. Many apple trees grow together in orchards.

Apple trees bloom in spring. The apples are picked in the fall.

Believe it or not, the apple and the rose are from the same plant family!

Apples are grown all over the world. Japan, Turkey, Poland and many other countries grow apples.

Most apples are still picked by hand! Many people enjoy picking apples in the fall for fun.

Apples are often made into juice called cider. You can drink cider hot or cold.

Apples can be baked into pies, cooked into applesauce, and made into jam.

Apples are very good for you. They are also tasty!

# Read More

Gleisner, Jenna Lee. *Apple Harvest*. North Mankato, MN: Child's World, 2017.

Oldfield, Dawn Bluemel. *Apple*. New York, NY: Bearport Publishing, 2016.

Saunders-Smith, Gail. *Apple Trees*. North Mankato, MN: Capstone Press, 2016.

# Websites

**Science for Kids**

*www.scienceforkidsclub.com/apples.html*
Learn more about apples.

**Science Kids**

*www.sciencekids.co.nz/sciencefacts/food/apples.html*
Read facts about apples.

# Index

Guided Reading Level: A
Guided Reading Leveling System is based on the guidelines recommended by Fountas and Pinnell.

Word Count: 131